# Ineffabilis A Systematic Analysis of Apocryphal Literature & Critique of Non-Canonical Texts

Anthony Brown

Published by Kvng Leo Publications, 2023.

While every precaution has been taken in the preparation of this book, the publisher assumes no responsibility for errors or omissions, or for damages resulting from the use of the information contained herein.

INEFFABILIS A SYSTEMATIC ANALYSIS OF APOCRYPHAL LITERATURE & CRITIQUE OF NON-CANONICAL TEXTS

**First edition. March 8, 2023.**



ISBN: 979-8224224401

Written by Anthony Brown.

# Table of Contents


Ineffabilis A Systematic Analysis of Apocryphal Literature & Critique of Non-Canonical Texts ....................1

Chapter 1 Introudction ....................3

chapter 2 The Gospel of Thomas ....................7

Chapter 3 Gospel of Judas ....................15

Chapter 4 The gospel of Thomas & the Acts of Peter ....................21

Chapter 5 The childhood of Jesus ....................31

Chapter 6 The Gospel of Pseudo-Matthew ....................35

Chapter 7 The gospel of Mary ....................39

Chapter 8 women & Ordiination ....................47

Chapter 9 The "holy quran" and Jesus ....................49

Chapter 10 The Unchanged canon ....................51

Chapter 11 Similarities between Hindu and the Cannon ....................55

Chapter 12 Similarities Between Ancient Egypt & Christianity ...57

Chapter 13 Revelation of God ....................61

Chapter 14 Conclusion ....................65

**Dedicaton**

I dedicate this book to my father, Andrew Brown Sr. He was one of the most brilliant pastor, preacher, theologian, father that I have ever known. He is truly missed.

# Foreward

The term "ineffable" refers to something that is too great, powerful, or sacred to be adequately expressed or described in words. It is often used to describe experiences or feelings that are beyond ordinary human expression, such as mystical or spiritual experiences. The word "ineffable" comes from the Latin "ineffabilis," which means "unutterable" or "unspeakable." This book is a scholarly critique of why non-canonical texts are excluded from the biblical canon might involve examining factors such as the texts' historical and cultural context, their authorship and authenticity, their theological and doctrinal consistency with other accepted texts, and their widespread use and acceptance among early Christian communities. The exclusion of certain texts from the biblical canon was a complex process that took place over many centuries, and involved a range of factors, including political considerations, theological disputes, and cultural and linguistic differences. This scholarly critique of non-canonical texts considers these and other factors in order to understand why they were not included in the canon. Finally, we hypothesize and give a critique of what this means to the universal world.

# Chapter 1 Introudction

## Lost books of the bible

The Lost Books of the Bible, also known as the Apocrypha or the Deuterocanonical books, are a collection of texts that were not included in the biblical canon recognized by most mainstream Christian denominations. These texts were written during the same time period as the books of the Old and New Testaments, but were not included in the official canon because they were not considered to be divinely inspired.

The Lost Books of the Bible contain a variety of genres, including historical accounts, poetry, wisdom literature, and apocalyptic visions. Some of the most well-known texts include the Gospel of Thomas, the Book of Enoch, and the Apocalypse of Peter. These texts were highly valued by early Christian communities, and were often read alongside the canonical texts in worship services and private study.

Despite their popularity, the Lost Books of the Bible were excluded from the official canon due to a variety of reasons. Some texts were rejected because they were deemed to be heretical or at odds with the teachings of the church. Others were excluded because they were not widely recognized as authoritative, or because they were written too late to be considered part of the original canon.[1]

Despite their exclusion, the Lost Books of the Bible continue to be studied and appreciated by many scholars and laypeople alike. These texts offer valuable insights into the religious and cultural contexts in which they were written, and provide a deeper understanding of the diversity of beliefs and practices that existed within early Christianity.

For example, the Gospel of Thomas contains a collection of sayings attributed to Jesus, some of which are similar to those found in the canonical Gospels, while others are more esoteric and mystical in nature. The Book of Enoch describes the adventures of the biblical figure Enoch, who is taken up to heaven and given visions of the end of the world. The

Apocalypse of Peter offers a vivid and terrifying account of the afterlife and the punishments that await sinners.

Some denominations, such as the Roman Catholic and Eastern Orthodox churches, include additional books in the Old Testament that are not found in Protestant Bibles. These books are known as the "deuterocanonical" books (from the Greek words "second" and "canon"). The deuterocanonical books are considered part of the canon by some Christian denominations, but not by others.

The deuterocanonical books, also known as the Apocrypha, include such texts as Tobit, Judith, Wisdom of Solomon, Sirach (Ecclesiasticus), Baruch, and 1 and 2 Maccabees. These texts were written in the same time period as the other books of the Old Testament, and were included in the Septuagint, a Greek translation of the Hebrew Scriptures that was widely used in the early Christian church.[2]

The inclusion of the deuterocanonical books in the Old Testament canon has been a point of controversy among different Christian denominations. Protestants generally reject the deuterocanonical books, arguing that they were not included in the Jewish canon and were not cited by Jesus or the New Testament writers. They also point to some doctrinal differences between the deuterocanonical books and the rest of the Old Testament.

On the other hand, the Roman Catholic and Eastern Orthodox churches accept the deuterocanonical books as part of the canon, viewing them as authoritative and inspired scripture. [3]These churches point to the fact that the deuterocanonical books were widely used and accepted by early Christians, and that they provide important insights into Jewish history and religious practices.

Despite these differences, it is important to recognize that the various Christian denominations share a common faith in the same God and the same Savior, and that their disagreements over the canon of scripture do not negate their shared beliefs and values. Regardless of which books are included in the canon, the Bible remains a powerful source of spiritual guidance and inspiration for millions of people around the world.

While the Lost Books of the Bible are not considered to be part of the official canon by most Christian denominations, they continue to be read and appreciated by many people today. These texts offer a fascinating glimpse into the religious and cultural worlds of the past, and provide valuable insights into the beliefs and practices of early Christians. Whether they are studied for their historical or spiritual significance, the Lost Books of the Bible remain an important part of the Christian literary tradition.

# chapter 2 The Gospel of Thomas

### Who wrote the Gospel of Thomas?

The Gospel of Thomas is a collection of 114 sayings attributed to Jesus that is believed to have been written in the early 2nd century. The author of the Gospel of Thomas is not known, and the text does not indicate who wrote it. The Gospel of Thomas is not included in the canon of any Christian denomination, and it is not considered to be part of the Bible. However, it is considered to be a significant text in the study of early Christianity, and it is often studied alongside the New Testament gospels in order to understand the diversity of early Christian thought. The Gospel of Thomas is written in Coptic, an Egyptian language that was used in the early Christian church, and it is thought to have been based on a Greek version of the text that has not survived.

### What are the 114 says attributed to Jesus that are in the Gospel of Thomas?

The Gospel of Thomas is a collection of 114 sayings attributed to Jesus that are organized into a series of short, independent units. The sayings in the Gospel of Thomas are not arranged in a narrative format like the gospels in the New Testament, and they do not tell the story of Jesus' life, ministry, death, or resurrection. Instead, they are more like a collection of wise sayings or teachings that are attributed to Jesus. Some of the sayings in the Gospel of Thomas are similar to sayings that are found in the New Testament gospels, while others are unique to the Gospel of Thomas. Here are a few examples of the sayings that are found in the Gospel of Thomas:

"The kingdom of the Father is spread out upon the earth, and people do not see it." (Saying 3)

"If you bring forth what is within you, what you bring forth will save you. If you do not bring forth what is within you, what you do not bring forth will destroy you." (Saying 70)

"Do not be afraid of those who kill the body but cannot kill the soul. Rather, be afraid of the one who can destroy both soul and body in hell." (Saying 75)

"Let him who seeks continue seeking until he finds. When he finds, he will become troubled. When he becomes troubled, he will be astonished, and he will rule over the All." (Saying 2)

"I am not your master. Because you have drunk, you have become drunk from the bubbling spring that I have tended." (Saying 13)

"The Father's kingdom is like a woman. She took a little leaven, hid it in dough, and made it into large loaves of bread. Anyone here with two ears had better listen!" (Saying 96)

These are just a few examples of the sayings that are found in the Gospel of Thomas. The text is known for its enigmatic and often cryptic language, and many of the sayings are open to multiple interpretations.[4]

The Gospel of Thomas is a non-canonical text that contains 114 sayings attributed to Jesus Christ. These sayings provide insights into the teachings of Jesus and have been a topic of interest among scholars and theologians for several decades. In this essay, we will explore the significance of the 114 sayings of the Gospel of Thomas.

Firstly, the Gospel of Thomas offers a unique perspective on the teachings of Jesus. Unlike the canonical gospels, which provide a narrative of Jesus' life and ministry, the Gospel of Thomas consists solely of sayings attributed to Jesus. This allows readers to focus solely on the teachings of Jesus, without the distraction of a narrative. Moreover, the sayings in the Gospel of Thomas are often presented in a poetic and cryptic manner, which encourages readers to contemplate their meaning deeply.

Secondly, the Gospel of Thomas provides insight into the early Christian community. The Gospel of Thomas was likely written in the first century, around the same time as the canonical gospels. The sayings in the Gospel of Thomas demonstrate that there were different interpretations of Jesus' teachings within the early Christian community. The Gospel of Thomas also highlights the diversity of early Christian beliefs and practices, which were not necessarily unified or homogenous.

Thirdly, the Gospel of Thomas challenges traditional Christian beliefs. Some of the sayings in the Gospel of Thomas contradict traditional Christian teachings, such as the idea of original sin or the concept of salvation through faith in Jesus. For example, Saying 70 of the Gospel of Thomas states that "If you bring forth what is within you, what you bring forth will save you. If you do not bring forth what is within you, what you do not bring forth will destroy you." This saying suggests that salvation comes from within, rather than from external sources such as faith in Jesus.

Fourthly, the Gospel of Thomas emphasizes the importance of self-discovery and self-knowledge. Many of the sayings in the Gospel of Thomas encourage readers to look within themselves for answers and guidance. For example, Saying 3 of the Gospel of Thomas states that "If your leaders say to you, 'Look, the kingdom is in the sky,' then the birds of the sky will precede you. If they say to you, 'It is in the sea,' then the fish will precede you. Rather, the kingdom is inside of you, and it is outside of you." This saying suggests that the key to understanding the kingdom of God is to look within oneself, rather than to rely on external authorities.

Finally, the Gospel of Thomas inspires readers to seek knowledge and understanding. The cryptic and poetic nature of the sayings in the Gospel of Thomas encourages readers to contemplate and interpret their meaning. This process of interpretation and reflection can lead to greater knowledge and understanding of Jesus' teachings and their relevance to our lives today.

The 114 sayings of the Gospel of Thomas are significant for several reasons. They offer a unique perspective on the teachings of Jesus, provide insight into the early Christian community, challenge traditional Christian beliefs, emphasize the importance of self-discovery and self-knowledge, and inspire readers to seek knowledge and understanding. As such, the Gospel of Thomas remains a valuable resource for scholars, theologians, and anyone interested in exploring the teachings of Jesus.

**Does the Gospel of Thomas remind you of Buddhist beliefs?**

The Gospel of Thomas is a collection of sayings attributed to Jesus, discovered in 1945 near Nag Hammadi, Egypt. As explained, the text is not considered a part of the Christian biblical canon and is widely believed to be a Gnostic work. There has been much debate about the influence of Buddhism on early Christian texts, and the Gospel of Thomas is often cited as an example of this possible influence. In this essay, I will examine whether the Gospel of Thomas reminds me of Buddhist beliefs.[5]

Firstly, the Gospel of Thomas contains many sayings that are similar to Buddhist teachings. For example, saying 27 in the Gospel of Thomas states: "If you do not fast as regards the world, you will not find the kingdom. If you do not observe the Sabbath as a Sabbath, you will not see the father." This saying appears to suggest that one needs to detach oneself from the material world in order to reach a higher spiritual state. This concept is similar to the Buddhist idea of detachment, which involves letting go of attachment to the physical world in order to achieve enlightenment.[6]

Similarly, saying 42 in the Gospel of Thomas states: "Be passersby." This saying suggests that one should not become too attached to any particular place or situation, but rather should move through life with detachment. This idea is similar to the Buddhist concept of impermanence, which holds that everything in life is constantly changing and that one should not become too attached to any particular thing or situation.[7]

In addition to these similarities in specific sayings, there are also broader themes in the Gospel of Thomas that are similar to Buddhist beliefs. For example, the Gospel of Thomas emphasizes the importance of direct experience of the divine, rather than relying on an intermediary such as a priest or religious institution. This is similar to the Buddhist idea of relying on personal experience and direct realization of the truth, rather than relying on external authority.

Furthermore, the Gospel of Thomas emphasizes the importance of inner transformation and self-knowledge. This is similar to the Buddhist concept of self-awareness and the importance of developing one's own wisdom and understanding of the nature of reality.

However, it is important to note that there are also significant differences between the Gospel of Thomas and Buddhist beliefs. For example, the Gospel of Thomas emphasizes the importance of faith in Jesus as a savior figure, which is not a concept found in Buddhism. Additionally, the Gospel of Thomas contains many references to the Jewish scriptures and traditions, which are not part of Buddhist teachings.

While there are similarities between the Gospel of Thomas and Buddhist beliefs, it is important to recognize that these similarities are not necessarily evidence of direct influence. It is possible that these similarities arise from a common human search for spiritual truth and the nature of reality. Nonetheless, the similarities suggest that there may be some shared themes and values between different religious traditions.

### Was there a political agenda in the Gospel of Thomas?

While the authorship of the Gospel of Thomas is still a matter of debate, it is generally agreed that the text was written by a group of early Christians who were influenced by Gnostic thought. There is no evidence to suggest that Thomas, the disciple of Jesus, had a political agenda, as he is not mentioned in the text.

Theologians have various interpretations of the agenda behind the Gospel of Thomas. Some argue that the text was written to preserve the teachings of Jesus in a form that was accessible to a wider audience than the canonical gospels, which were written in Greek and intended for a predominantly Jewish audience. The Gospel of Thomas was likely written in Coptic, which was the language spoken in Egypt at the time, and may have been intended for a broader audience.[8]

Others argue that the Gospel of Thomas was written to promote a particular form of Gnostic Christianity. Gnosticism was a religious movement that emphasized the importance of knowledge and personal experience of the divine. Gnostics believed that the material world was corrupt and that salvation could only be achieved through knowledge of the divine. Some of the sayings in the Gospel of Thomas reflect Gnostic beliefs, such as Saying 70, which suggests that salvation comes from within.

Still, others argue that the Gospel of Thomas was written as a response to the challenges faced by the early Christian community. The Gospel of Thomas was likely written in the first century, a time of political and social upheaval in the Roman Empire. Some theologians argue that the Gospel of Thomas was written to provide guidance and encouragement to the early Christian community, which faced persecution and marginalization.

Overall, there is no evidence to suggest that the author of the Gospel of Thomas, whoever they may have been, had a political agenda. The text is primarily concerned with preserving the teachings of Jesus and promoting a particular form of early Christian thought, which emphasized the importance of knowledge and personal experience of the divine. While the Gospel of Thomas may have been written in response to the challenges faced by the early Christian community, its primary agenda was religious and theological, rather than political.

**What would have made the Gospel of Thomas accepted in the Canon?**

The Gospel of Thomas is a non-canonical text that contains a collection of sayings attributed to Jesus. Unlike the canonical gospels, which provide a narrative of Jesus' life and ministry, the Gospel of

Thomas consists solely of these sayings. The Gospel of Thomas was not included in the canon of the New Testament, which is a collection of books recognized by the Christian Church as authoritative and inspired by God. W]e will explore what would have made the Gospel of Thomas accepted in the canon.[9]

Firstly, the Gospel of Thomas would have needed to have been written by one of the apostles or a close associate of Jesus. The canon of the New Testament includes books that were written by apostles or their associates, such as the Gospel of Matthew, which was written by the apostle Matthew, [10]and the Gospel of Mark, which was written by the associate of the apostle Peter. The Gospel of Thomas was likely not written by an apostle or their associate, which would have made it difficult for it to be accepted into the canon.

Secondly, the Gospel of Thomas would have needed to be consistent with the teachings of the apostles and the early Church. The canon of the New Testament includes books that are consistent with the teachings of the apostles and the early Church, such as the letters of Paul, which provide guidance to the early Christian communities. The Gospel of Thomas contains some sayings that are consistent with the teachings of the apostles and the early Church, but it also contains some sayings that contradict traditional Christian beliefs.

Thirdly, the Gospel of Thomas would have needed to have been widely accepted and used by the early Christian communities. The canon of the New Testament includes books that were widely accepted and used by the early Christian communities, such as the Gospels of Matthew, Mark, Luke, and John. The Gospel of Thomas was not widely accepted or used by the early Christian communities, which would have made it difficult for it to be included in the canon.

Finally, the Gospel of Thomas would have needed to have been recognized and approved by the early Church councils. The canon of the New Testament was not formally established until the fourth century, when the Councils of Hippo and Carthage recognized a list of books as authoritative and inspired by God. The Gospel of Thomas was not included in the list of books recognized by these councils, which would have made it difficult for it to be included in the canon.

There are several factors that would have made the Gospel of Thomas accepted in the canon. The Gospel of Thomas would have needed to have been written by an apostle or their associate, consistent with the teachings of the apostles and the early Church, widely accepted and used by the early Christian communities, and recognized and approved by the early Church councils. While the Gospel of Thomas did not meet these criteria, it remains an important and valuable resource for scholars and theologians interested in the early Christian movement and the teachings of Jesus.

# Chapter 3 Gospel of Judas

## Summary of the Gospel of Judas

The Gospel of Judas is a text that purports to be written by Judas Iscariot, one of the disciples of Jesus, and it presents a different interpretation of the relationship between Jesus and Judas than the one found in the New Testament. The Gospel of Judas is not included in the canon of any Christian denomination, and it is not considered to be part of the Bible. However, it is considered to be a significant text in the study of early Christianity, and it has generated a lot of interest and controversy due to its unique perspective on the role of Judas in the story of Jesus.[11]

According to the Gospel of Judas, Judas was the only one of the disciples who truly understood the teachings of Jesus and the nature of his mission. The other disciples, including Peter and the other apostles, misunderstood Jesus and misinterpreted his teachings. Judas, on the other hand, was favored by Jesus and was given special knowledge and insight into the true nature of his mission.[12]

In the Gospel of Judas, Jesus is depicted as a divine being who came to earth to reveal the true nature of God to humanity. He tells Judas that he has been chosen to be the "thirteenth spirit," and that he will be the one to "sacrifice the man that clothes me." This has been interpreted by some as a reference to the betrayal of Jesus by Judas, as described in the New Testament.

The Gospel of Judas also includes teachings and parables that are similar to those found in the New Testament gospels, but with a different emphasis and interpretation. For example, the parable of the sower is interpreted as a

metaphor for the way in which the teachings of Jesus are received by different people.

The Gospel of Judas presents a different perspective on the story of Jesus and the role of Judas in the events leading up to his death. It is a complex and enigmatic text that has generated much debate and discussion among scholars and theologians.

### What parables are in the Gospel of Judas?

The Gospel of Judas includes several parables that are similar to those found in the New Testament gospels, but with a different emphasis and interpretation. Here are a few examples of the parables that are found in the Gospel of Judas:

The Parable of the Sower: This parable, which is also found in the New Testament gospels of Matthew, Mark, and Luke, is interpreted in the Gospel of Judas as a metaphor for the way in which the teachings of Jesus are received by different people.[13]

The Parable of the Wheat and the Weeds: This parable, which is also found in the New Testament gospel of Matthew, is interpreted in the Gospel of Judas as a metaphor for the way in which the teachings of Jesus will eventually triumph over the forces of evil.

The Parable of the Mustard Seed: This parable, which is also found in the New Testament gospels of Matthew and Luke, is interpreted in the Gospel of Judas as a metaphor for the way in which the kingdom of God will grow and spread throughout the world.

Overall, the parables in the Gospel of Judas are similar to those found in the New Testament gospels, but they are interpreted in a different way, with a focus on the teachings of Jesus and the role of Judas in the story of Jesus.

### How are the parables different in the Gospel of Judas?

The parables in the Gospel of Judas are similar to those found in the New Testament gospels, but they are interpreted in a different way, with a focus on the teachings of Jesus and the role of Judas in the story of Jesus.[14]

One difference between the parables in the Gospel of Judas and those in the New Testament gospels is that the parables in the Gospel of Judas are often interpreted more allegorically, with a focus on the deeper meanings and teachings that are conveyed by the parables. For example, the parable of the sower, which is also found in the New Testament gospels of Matthew, Mark, and Luke, is interpreted in the Gospel of Judas as a metaphor for the way in which the teachings of Jesus are received by different people.

Another difference is that the parables in the Gospel of Judas often have a more eschatological (end-times) focus, with a emphasis on the eventual triumph of the kingdom of God over the forces of evil. For example, the parable of the wheat and the weeds, which is also found in the New Testament gospel of Matthew, is interpreted in the Gospel of Judas as a metaphor for the way in which the teachings of Jesus will eventually triumph over the forces of evil.

Overall, the parables in the Gospel of Judas are similar to those found in the New Testament gospels, but they are interpreted in a different way, with a focus on the teachings of Jesus and the role of Judas in the story of Jesus.

**How did the other disciples misunderstand Jesus teachings and Judas have a better understanding of the nature of Jesus teachings?**

In the Gospel of Judas, Jesus is depicted as a divine being who came to earth to reveal the true nature of God to humanity. He tells Judas that he has been chosen to be the "thirteenth spirit," and that he will be the one to "sacrifice the man that clothes me." This has been interpreted by some as a reference to the betrayal of Jesus by Judas, as described in the New Testament.

The Gospel of Judas also includes teachings and parables that are similar to those found in the New Testament gospels, but with a different emphasis and interpretation. For example, the parable of the sower is interpreted as a metaphor for the way in which the teachings of Jesus are received by different people.

The Gospel of Judas presents a different perspective on the story of Jesus and the role of Judas in the events leading up to his death. It is a complex and enigmatic text that has generated much debate and discussion among scholars and theologians.[15]

**What was the political agenda of the writer of the gospel of Judas?**

The Gospel of Judas is a text from the early Christian era that was discovered in Egypt in the 1970s. The text presents an alternative version of the events leading up to the crucifixion of Jesus Christ, one in which Judas is portrayed in a more sympathetic light than in the canonical gospels. While the identity of the author of the Gospel of Judas is not known for certain, scholars have suggested that the text reflects a particular political agenda.

One of the key features of the Gospel of Judas is its portrayal of Judas as a loyal disciple of Jesus who was given a special mission to hand him over to the authorities. According to the text, Jesus chose Judas for this task because he was the only one among the disciples who had the necessary spiritual insight to understand the true nature of Jesus' mission. By handing Jesus over to the authorities, Judas was not betraying him but rather fulfilling his destiny.

This interpretation of Judas' actions stands in stark contrast to the version presented in the canonical gospels, where Judas is portrayed as a traitor who betrayed Jesus for money. The Gospel of Judas thus challenges the orthodox Christian view of Judas and presents a more sympathetic portrayal of him.

Some scholars have suggested that the political agenda behind the Gospel of Judas was to promote a particular form of Gnosticism, a religious movement that emphasized secret knowledge and mystical experiences as the key to spiritual salvation. According to this theory, the Gospel of Judas was written by a Gnostic group that wanted to present their version of Christianity as the true and authentic one.

In this interpretation, the portrayal of Judas as a spiritual hero was intended to challenge the orthodox Christian view of salvation, which emphasized faith in Jesus as the only path to redemption. By presenting Judas as a figure who was chosen by Jesus himself for a special mission, the Gospel of Judas sought to elevate the importance of secret knowledge and spiritual insight in the quest for salvation.

Another possible political agenda of the Gospel of Judas was to challenge the authority of the early Christian church. The text was likely written during a time of great turmoil and sectarian conflict within the early Christian movement, and some scholars have suggested that the author of the Gospel of Judas was a member of a group that had been marginalized or even persecuted by the orthodox church.

By presenting an alternative version of the events leading up to the crucifixion of Jesus, the Gospel of Judas may have been intended to challenge the authority and legitimacy of the orthodox church. The portrayal of Judas as a spiritual hero and the emphasis on secret knowledge and mystical experiences could be seen as a way of subverting the authority of the church and promoting an alternative form of Christianity.

While the identity of the author of the Gospel of Judas remains unknown, scholars have suggested that the text reflects a particular political agenda. The portrayal of Judas as a spiritual hero and the emphasis on secret knowledge and mystical experiences may have been intended to promote a particular form of Gnosticism or to challenge the authority of the early Christian church. The Gospel of Judas thus provides a fascinating glimpse into the complex and contested world of early Christians

# Chapter 4 The gospel of Thomas & the Acts of Peter

There are many sayings in the Gospel of Thomas.

Saying 1: "These are the hidden words that the living Jesus spoke, and Didymos Judas Thomas wrote them down."

The Gospel of Thomas is a collection of 114 sayings attributed to Jesus that is believed to have been written in the early 2nd century. The sayings in the Gospel of Thomas are not arranged in a narrative format like the gospels in the New Testament, and they do not tell the story of Jesus' life, ministry, death, or resurrection. Instead, they are more like a collection of wise sayings or teachings that are attributed to Jesus. The text is known for its enigmatic and often cryptic language, and many of the sayings are open to multiple interpretations.[16]

Saying 1 introduces the text and indicates that the sayings contained in it are the words of Jesus, as recorded by Didymos Judas Thomas. The identity of Didymos Judas Thomas is not certain, but he is traditionally believed to be the apostle Thomas, one of the twelve apostles of Jesus. The text does not indicate when or where the sayings were recorded, or the circumstances under which they were spoken.[17]

What is the Apocalypse of Peter in Detail?

The is a text that describes a vision of the afterlife and the end of the world.

The Apocalypse of Peter is a text that describes a vision of the afterlife and the end of the world that is believed to have been written in the 2nd century. The text is not included in the canon of any Christian denomination, and it is not considered to be part of the Bible. However, it is considered to be a significant text in the study of early Christianity, and it has been the subject of much debate and discussion among scholars and theologians.[18]

According to the Apocalypse of Peter, the text describes a vision that was given to the apostle Peter by Jesus, in which he was shown the wonders of heaven and the horrors of hell. In the vision, Peter sees the souls of the righteous being rewarded in heaven, while the souls of the wicked are punished in hell.[19]

The Apocalypse of Peter also includes a description of the end of the world, in which the earth will be destroyed and the dead will be resurrected. The text suggests that there will be a final judgment, in which the souls of the dead will be judged according to their deeds, and that those who are found worthy will be rewarded with eternal life in heaven.[20]

The Apocalypse of Peter is a complex and enigmatic text that presents a unique perspective on the afterlife and the end of the world. It is important to note that the text is not considered to be a reliable historical source, and that its depiction of the afterlife and the end of the world should not be taken as definitive or authoritative.

Is the Apocalypse of Peter similar to the book of Revelations?

The Apocalypse of Peter is a text that describes a vision of the afterlife and the end of the world that is believed to have been written in the 2nd century. The Book of Revelation, also known as the Apocalypse of John, is a book of the New Testament that describes a series of visions and prophecies that are believed to have been received by the apostle John on the island of Patmos. The Apocalypse of Peter and the Book of Revelation are similar in that both texts describe visions of the end of the world and the afterlife, and both texts include imagery and symbolism that is meant to convey the grandeur and importance of these events.

However, there are also some significant differences between the Apocalypse of Peter and the Book of Revelation. The Apocalypse of Peter is not considered to be part of the canon of any Christian denomination, and it is not considered to be part of the Bible. The Book of Revelation, on the other hand, is considered to be part of the canon of the Christian Bible, and it is considered to be a reliable and authoritative source for the teachings of the Christian faith.

Additionally, the Apocalypse of Peter and the Book of Revelation differ in their content and the specific details of their descriptions of the end of the world and the afterlife. The Apocalypse of Peter describes a vision that was given to the apostle Peter by Jesus, while the Book of Revelation describes a series of visions that were received by the apostle John. The Apocalypse of Peter also includes a description of the final judgment, in which the souls of the dead will be judged according to their deeds, while the Book of Revelation describes the final victory of God over evil and the establishment of the kingdom of God on earth.[21]

Overall, while the Apocalypse of Peter and the Book of Revelation are similar in some ways, they are also distinct texts that present different perspectives on the end of the world and the afterlife.

In The Acts of Peter: This is a text that describes the teachings and miracles of Peter, one of the apostles of Jesus, What are the teachings and miracles of Peter in more detail?[22]

The Acts of Peter is a text that purports to describe the teachings and miracles of Peter, one of the apostles of Jesus. The text is not considered to be part of the canon of any Christian denomination, and it is not considered to be a reliable historical source for the life and teachings of Peter. However, it is considered to be a significant text in the study of early Christianity, and it has been the subject of much debate and discussion among scholars and theologians.

The Acts of Peter includes a number of stories and accounts of the teachings and miracles of Peter. Some of the teachings and miracles described in the text include:

Preaching and evangelizing: The Acts of Peter describes Peter as an enthusiastic and powerful preacher who was able to convert many people to the Christian faith.

Healing the sick: The text describes Peter as having the power to heal the sick and perform miracles. In one story, he is said to have raised a young boy from the dead.

Exorcising demons: The Acts of Peter also describes Peter as having the ability to exorcise demons from possessed individuals.

Defying death: In one story, Peter is said to have been thrown to the lions by the Roman authorities, but he was able to escape unharmed and converted many of the lions to Christianity.

The Acts of Peter is a text that presents a legendary and sometimes fantastical account of the teachings and miracles of Peter. It is important to note that the text is not considered to be a reliable historical source, and that its depiction of the teachings and miracles of Peter should not be taken as definitive or authoritative.

What is in detail The Acts of Peter?

The text that describes the teachings and miracles of Peter, one of the apostles of Jesus, in more detail

The Acts of Peter is a text that purports to describe the teachings and miracles of Peter, one of the apostles of Jesus. The text is not considered to be part of the canon of any Christian denomination, and it is not considered to be a reliable historical source for the life and teachings of Peter. However, it is considered to be a significant text in the study of early Christianity, and it has been the subject of much debate and discussion among scholars and theologians.

The Acts of Peter includes a number of stories and accounts of the teachings and miracles of Peter. Some of the teachings and miracles described in the text include:

Preaching and evangelizing: The Acts of Peter describes Peter as an enthusiastic and powerful preacher who was able to convert many people to the Christian faith. In one story, he is said to have preached to a large crowd in Rome and convinced many of them to be baptized.

What is in detail The Acts of Paul?

# INEFFABILIS A SYSTEMATIC ANALYSIS OF APOCRYPHAL LITERATURE & CRITIQUE OF NON-CANONICAL TEXTS

This is a text that describes the teachings and miracles of Paul, one of the apostles of Jesus.

The Acts of Paul is a text that purports to describe the teachings and miracles of Paul, one of the apostles of Jesus. The text is not considered to be part of the canon of any Christian denomination, and it is not considered to be a reliable historical source for the life and teachings of Paul. However, it is considered to be a significant text in the study of early Christianity, and it has been the subject of much debate and discussion among scholars and theologians.

The Acts of Paul includes a number of stories and accounts of the teachings and miracles of Paul. Some of the teachings and miracles described in the text include:

Preaching and evangelizing: The Acts of Paul describes Paul as an enthusiastic and powerful preacher who was able to convert many people to the Christian faith. In one story, he is said to have preached to a large crowd in Corinth and convinced many of them to be baptized.

Healing the sick: The text describes Paul as having the power to heal the sick and perform miracles. In one story, he is said to have healed a woman who was suffering from a severe illness by simply laying his hands on her.

Exorcising demons: The Acts of Paul also describes Paul as having the ability to exorcise demons from possessed individuals. In one story, he is said to have exorcised a demon from a young boy who was possessed by a "legion" of demons.

Defying death: In one story, Paul is said to have survived a shipwreck and been rescued by an angel. In another story, he is said to have been arrested and imprisoned, but he was able to escape and continue his ministry.

The Acts of Paul is a text that presents a legendary and sometimes fantastical account of the teachings and miracles of Paul. It is important to note that the text is not considered to be a reliable historical source, and that its depiction of the teachings and miracles of Paul should not be taken as definitive or authoritative.

The acts of Peter and Paul seem similar. Are they written by the same author?

The Acts of Peter and The Acts of Paul are two texts that claim to describe the teachings and miracles of Peter and Paul, respectively, two of the apostles of Jesus. Both texts are considered to be significant in the study of early Christianity, but they are not considered to be part of the canon of any Christian denomination, and they are not considered to be reliable historical sources for the life and teachings of Peter and Paul.[23]

It is not known for certain who wrote The Acts of Peter and The Acts of Paul, or when they were written. Both texts are believed to have been written in the 2nd century, but the identities of their authors are not known. Some scholars have suggested that The Acts of Peter and The Acts of Paul may have been written by the same author, while others have argued that they were written by different authors.

The Acts of Peter and The Acts of Paul are similar in that they both contain accounts of the teachings and miracles of their respective apostles, and they both present a legendary and sometimes fantastical depiction of these events. However, they also contain some significant differences, and they should not be assumed to be written by the same author or to represent a consistent or unified viewpoint.

Overall, The Acts of Peter and The Acts of Paul are important texts in the study of early Christianity, but they should not be taken as reliable historical sources or as definitive accounts of the lives and teachings of Peter and Paul.

Is there any similarity between the acts of Peter and the acts of Paul with the Acts of the Apostles?

The Acts of the Apostles is a book of the New Testament that describes the activities and teachings of the apostles of Jesus, including Peter and Paul. The Acts of Peter and The Acts of Paul are texts that appear to describe the teachings and miracles of Peter and Paul, respectively, two of the apostles of Jesus, but they are not considered to be part of the canon of any Christian denomination, and they are not considered to be reliable historical sources for the life and teachings of Peter and Paul.

There is some similarity between the Acts of the Apostles and The Acts of Peter and The Acts of Paul in that they all describe the activities and teachings of the apostles of Jesus, including Peter and Paul. However, there are also significant differences between these texts. The Acts of the Apostles is considered to be part of the canon of the Christian Bible, and it is considered to be a reliable and authoritative source for the teachings of the Christian faith. The Acts of Peter and The Acts of Paul, on the other hand, are not considered to be part of the Bible, and they are not considered to be reliable historical sources.[24]

Additionally, the Acts of the Apostles presents a more comprehensive and historically reliable account of the activities and teachings of the apostles than The Acts of Peter and The Acts of Paul, which contain more legendary and fantastical elements. The Acts of the Apostles is believed to have been written by the apostle Luke, and it is based on the eyewitness testimony of the apostles and other early Christian believers. The Acts of Peter and The Acts of Paul, on the other hand, are believed to have been written by anonymous authors, and they present a more legendary and sometimes fantastical portrayal of the activities and teachings of the apostles.

While there is some similarity between the Acts of the Apostles, The Acts of Peter, and The Acts of Paul, they are distinct texts that present different perspectives on the activities and teachings of the apostles of Jesus. It is important to note that The Acts of Peter and The Acts of Paul are not considered to be reliable historical sources, and that their depictions of the

The Acts of Peter and the Acts of Paul are two apocryphal texts that are often studied together due to their similar themes and structures. Although they were not included in the canonical Bible, they were widely read and circulated in early Christian communities and provide valuable insights into the religious and cultural practices of the time.

The Acts of Peter is a narrative that describes the miraculous events that took place during Peter's ministry. The text begins with the story of a man named Simon Magus, who was a sorcerer and claimed to be a powerful magician. Peter challenges Simon Magus to a contest of miracles, and through divine intervention, Peter is able to perform incredible feats that demonstrate the power of God. The text also describes Peter's travels and missionary work, as well as his eventual martyrdom in Rome.

The Acts of Paul, on the other hand, follows a similar narrative structure but focuses on the life and ministry of the apostle Paul. The text describes the many miracles that Paul performed during his missionary work, as well as his conflicts with the authorities and his eventual martyrdom.

Both texts emphasize the power of faith and the importance of repentance and redemption. They depict the apostles as powerful figures who are able to perform miracles and heal the sick, and they emphasize the importance of following in their footsteps and living a righteous life. The texts also provide insight into the religious and cultural practices of the time, including the worship of pagan gods and the conflicts between early Christians and the Roman authorities.[25]

One notable aspect of both texts is their use of dramatic and sometimes fantastical storytelling techniques. For example, in the Acts of Peter, there is a scene in which a dog speaks and confesses its belief in God after witnessing Peter's miracles. Similarly, in the Acts of Paul, there is a scene in which Paul is swallowed by a giant sea creature and survives for three days before being rescued.

# INEFFABILIS A SYSTEMATIC ANALYSIS OF APOCRYPHAL LITERATURE & CRITIQUE OF NON-CANONICAL TEXTS

The Acts of Peter and the Acts of Paul are valuable sources of information for scholars and historians studying early Christianity. They provide insight into the religious beliefs and practices of the time, as well as the cultural and political context in which these beliefs emerged. While they may not have been included in the canonical Bible, they are still widely studied and appreciated for their literary and historical significance.

Political agenda on the acts of Peter and the Acts of Paul

It is difficult to identify a specific political agenda in the Acts of Peter and the Acts of Paul, as these texts were primarily intended to provide religious instruction and reinforce the faith of early Christian communities. However, it is possible to identify certain political themes and motifs that appear in these texts.

One of the key political themes that appears in both texts is the conflict between early Christians and the Roman authorities. Both Peter and Paul are depicted as being persecuted by the Roman government for their beliefs, and their eventual martyrdoms are portrayed as acts of defiance against an oppressive regime. These narratives may have served to inspire and encourage early Christians who were facing similar persecution.[26]

In addition, both texts emphasize the importance of living a righteous and virtuous life, even in the face of persecution and opposition. This emphasis on personal morality may have served a political function by encouraging early Christians to resist the corrupt and immoral practices of the Roman government.

Another political theme that appears in both texts is the power of faith to overcome adversity. Through their miracles and acts of divine intervention, Peter and Paul are shown to have the ability to overcome seemingly insurmountable obstacles and to convert even the most stubborn skeptics. This emphasis on the power of faith may have served to inspire and unify early Christian communities, and to encourage them to persevere in the face of persecution and opposition.

It is worth noting that the Acts of Peter and the Acts of Paul were written during a time of significant political and social upheaval in the Roman Empire. These texts may have served as a means of providing comfort and stability to early Christian communities by providing a sense of continuity and tradition in a rapidly changing world.

While the Acts of Peter and the Acts of Paul were not primarily intended to serve a political agenda, they do contain certain political themes and motifs that reflect the historical context in which they were written. These texts provide valuable insights into the religious and cultural practices of early Christian communities, as well as the political and social challenges they faced.

# Chapter 5 The childhood of Jesus

The gospels of Matthew, Mark, Luke, and John in the New Testament of the Bible contain accounts of the life, teachings, death, and resurrection of Jesus. These texts include some information about Jesus' childhood, although they do not provide a comprehensive or detailed account of this period of his life.

The gospel of Luke, in particular, includes some information about Jesus' childhood. According to the gospel of Luke, Jesus was born to Mary and Joseph in Bethlehem and was visited by shepherds and wise men. When Jesus was around the age of two, his family fled to Egypt to escape the persecution of King Herod. After Herod's death, they returned to their home in Nazareth.

The gospel of Luke also includes the story of the presentation of Jesus in the temple, in which Jesus was presented to God according to Jewish custom and was recognized as a special and holy child by the elderly prophet Simeon.

While the gospels provide some information about Jesus' childhood, they do not provide a detailed or comprehensive account of this period of his life. The gospels focus more on Jesus' ministry, teachings, and miracles, and on the events leading up to his death and resurrection.

**Which lost book of the bible give a comprehensive account of the period of Jesus life prior to the age of 12?**

There is no lost book of the Bible that provides a comprehensive account of the period of Jesus' life prior to the age of 12. The gospels of Matthew, Mark, Luke, and John in the New Testament of the Bible contain the only accounts of Jesus' life that are considered to be part of the canon of the Christian Bible. These texts include some information about Jesus' childhood, although they do not provide a comprehensive or detailed account of this period of his life.

There are some texts that are not considered to be part of the canon of the Christian Bible that appears to provide additional information about Jesus' life, including his childhood. These texts, often referred to as "lost gospels" or "apocryphal gospels," are not considered to be reliable historical sources, and they are not considered to be authoritative or definitive accounts of Jesus' life.

While there is some information about Jesus' childhood included in the gospels of the New Testament, there is no lost book of the Bible that provides a comprehensive account of this period of his life. The gospels focus more on Jesus' ministry, teachings, and miracles, and on the events leading up to his death and resurrection.

## Which apocryphal gospel give account to Jesus Childhood prior to age twelve?

There are several apocryphal gospels that claim to provide additional information about the life of Jesus, including his childhood. These texts are not considered to be part of the canon of the Christian Bible, and they are not considered to be reliable historical sources. They are often referred to as "lost gospels" or "apocryphal gospels" and are not considered to be authoritative or definitive accounts of Jesus' life.[27]

Some examples of apocryphal gospels that include information about Jesus' childhood include:

The Infancy Gospel of Thomas: This text appears to describe the childhood of Jesus and includes stories of his miraculous deeds as a young boy. It is not considered to be a reliable historical source, and its depiction of Jesus' childhood should not be taken as definitive or authoritative.[28]

The Gospel of James: This text includes a story about the birth and childhood of Jesus, including a description of the angel Gabriel's announcement to Mary and the circumstances of Jesus' birth. It is not considered to be a reliable historical source, and its depiction of Jesus' childhood should not be taken as definitive or authoritative.[29]

## The Gospel of Pseudo-Matthew

This text includes a story about the birth and childhood of Jesus, including a description of the angel Gabriel's announcement to Mary and the circumstances of Jesus' birth. It is not considered to be a reliable historical source, and its depiction of Jesus' childhood should not be taken as definitive or authoritative.[30]

While these apocryphal gospels may include some information about Jesus' childhood, they should not be considered to be reliable historical sources and their depictions of Jesus' childhood should not be taken as definitive or authoritative. The gospels of the New Testament are considered to be the most reliable sources of information about the life of Jesus.

### What does the infancy Gospel of Thomas say about Jesus childhood?

The Infancy Gospel of Thomas is a text that appears to describe the childhood of Jesus and includes stories of his miraculous deeds as a young boy. It is not considered to be a reliable historical source, and its depiction of Jesus' childhood should not be taken as definitive or authoritative.

According to the Infancy Gospel of Thomas, Jesus displayed supernatural powers and abilities from a very young age. For example, the text describes how, as a young child, Jesus was able to animate clay birds and make them fly, and how he was able to heal the sick and perform other miracles. The text also includes stories of Jesus getting into trouble with his parents and other adults, and of his interactions with other children.

Infancy Gospel of Thomas presents a legendary and fantastical portrayal of Jesus' childhood, and it should not be taken as a reliable or definitive account of this period of his life. The gospels of the New Testament, particularly the gospel of Luke, are considered to be the most reliable sources of information about the life of Jesus.

**What does the Gospel of James say about Jesus childhood?**

The Gospel of James is a text that appears to provide additional information about the life of Jesus, including his childhood. It is not considered to be a reliable historical source, and its depiction of Jesus' childhood should not be taken as definitive or authoritative.[31]

According to the Gospel of James, Jesus was born to Mary and Joseph in Bethlehem, and he was visited by shepherds and wise men. The text also includes a story about the circumstances of Jesus' birth, including the angel Gabriel's announcement to Mary and the announcement of Jesus' birth to Joseph in a dream. The Gospel of James also includes a description of Jesus' circumcision and presentation in the temple, according to Jewish custom.[32]

While the Gospel of James includes some information about Jesus' childhood, it should not be considered a reliable or definitive source of information about this period of his life. The gospels of the New Testament, particularly the gospel of Luke, are considered to be the most reliable sources of information about the life of Jesus

# Chapter 6 The Gospel of Pseudo-Matthew

The Gospel of Pseudo-Matthew is a text that purports to provide additional information about the life of Jesus, including his childhood. It is not considered to be a reliable historical source, and its depiction of Jesus' childhood should not be taken as definitive or authoritative.

According to the Gospel of Pseudo-Matthew, Jesus was born to Mary and Joseph in Bethlehem, and he was visited by shepherds and wise men. The text also includes a story about the circumstances of Jesus' birth, including the angel Gabriel's announcement to Mary and the announcement of Jesus' birth to Joseph in a dream. The Gospel of Pseudo-Matthew also includes a description of Jesus' circumcision and presentation in the temple, according to Jewish custom.

In addition to these stories, the Gospel of Pseudo-Matthew includes a number of other legendary and fantastical accounts of Jesus' childhood and early life, including stories of his miraculous deeds and interactions with other children.

While the Gospel of Pseudo-Matthew includes some information about Jesus' childhood, it should not be considered a reliable or definitive source of information about this period of his life. The gospels of the New Testament, particularly the gospel of Luke, are considered to be the most reliable sources of information about the life of Jesus.[33]

**Was the Pseudo-Mathew, the Gospel of James and the infancy Gospel of Thomas written by the same person?**

It is not known for certain who wrote the Pseudo-Matthew, the Gospel of James, and the Infancy Gospel of Thomas, or when these texts were written. These texts are not considered to be part of the canon of the Christian Bible, and they are not considered to be reliable historical sources for the life of Jesus. They are often referred to as "lost gospels" or "apocryphal gospels," and they are not considered to be authoritative or definitive accounts of Jesus' life.

Some scholars have suggested that the Pseudo-Matthew, the Gospel of James, and the Infancy Gospel of Thomas may have been written by the same author, while others have argued that they were written by different authors. It is not known for certain who wrote these texts or what their motivations were for writing them.

Overall, while the Pseudo-Matthew, the Gospel of James, and the Infancy Gospel of Thomas may include some information about the life of Jesus, they should not be considered reliable or definitive sources of information about his life, teachings, or miracles. The gospels of the New Testament, particularly the gospels of Matthew, Mark, Luke, and John, are considered to be the most reliable sources of information about the life of Jesus.

**Is there evidence that the Pseudo-Matthew, the Gospel of James, and the Infancy Gospel of Thomas uses Mark as a reference like the other synoptic Gospels in the cannon, Mathew, Mark, Luke?**

It is not known for certain whether the Pseudo-Matthew, the Gospel of James, and the Infancy Gospel of Thomas used the gospel of Mark as a reference or source when they were written. These texts are not considered to be part of the canon of the Christian Bible, and they are not considered to be reliable historical sources for the life of Jesus. They are often referred to as "lost gospels" or "apocryphal gospels," and they are not considered to be authoritative or definitive accounts of Jesus' life.

The gospels of Matthew, Mark, and Luke are known as the synoptic gospels because they contain many similarities in terms of their content and structure. Some scholars have argued that these gospels may have used each other as sources or references when they were written. However, it is not known for certain whether the Pseudo-Matthew, the Gospel of James, and the Infancy Gospel of Thomas used the synoptic gospels as sources or references when they were written.

It is possible that the Pseudo-Matthew, the Gospel of James, and the Infancy Gospel of Thomas may have used the synoptic gospels as sources or references; however, there is no definitive evidence to support this claim. These texts should not be considered reliable or definitive sources of information about the life of Jesus, and they should not be taken as authoritative accounts of his teachings or miracles. The gospels of the New Testament, particularly the gospels of Matthew, Mark, Luke, and John, are considered to be the most reliable sources of information about the life of Jesus

# Chapter 7 The gospel of Mary

## Why is the Gospel of Mary in the Koran not in the Holy Bible (Cannon)?

The Gospel of Mary is not included in the Bible or the Koran. The Gospel of Mary is a non-canonical text that appears to provide additional information about the life of Jesus and the teachings of the early Christian church. It is not considered to be a reliable historical source, and it is not considered to be part of the canon of the Christian Bible.[34]

The canon of the Christian Bible refers to the texts that are considered to be authoritative and definitive accounts of the life and teachings of Jesus and the early Christian church. The canon of the Christian Bible includes the Old Testament, which is the Hebrew Bible, and the New Testament, which contains the gospels of Matthew, Mark, Luke, and John, as well as other texts that describe the teachings and activities of Jesus and the early Christian church.

The Gospel of Mary is not included in the canon of the Christian Bible because it is not considered to be a reliable or authoritative source of information about the life and teachings of Jesus and the early Christian church. It is not considered to be a genuine account of the life and teachings of Jesus, and it is not considered to be a reliable historical source.

The Gospel of Mary is not included in the canon of the Christian Bible because it is not considered to be a reliable or authoritative source of information about the life and teachings of Jesus and the early Christian church. The gospels of the New Testament, particularly the gospels of Matthew, Mark, Luke, and John, are considered to be the most reliable sources of information about the life of Jesus.

The Koran, on the other hand, is the holy book of Islam and is not related to the Christian New Testament canon. The Koran mentions

Mary, the mother of Jesus, but it does not include the Gospel of Mary or any other non-canonical Christian texts.

It's worth noting that the process of selecting which texts would be included in the Christian New Testament canon was a complex and lengthy one, with various texts being considered and debated by early Christian leaders. Ultimately, the texts that were included in the canon were those that were believed to be divinely inspired and in alignment with orthodox Christian teachings.

**What is the summary of the Gospel of Mary?**

The Gospel of Mary is a non-canonical text that purports to provide additional information about the life of Jesus and the teachings of the early Christian church. It is not considered to be a reliable historical source, and it is not considered to be part of the canon of the Christian Bible.

The text of the Gospel of Mary consists of a series of dialogues between Jesus and his disciples, as well as a series of visions and revelations that are experienced by Mary Magdalene. In these dialogues, Jesus teaches his disciples about the nature of the soul and the importance of spiritual knowledge and understanding. He also encourages them to follow his teachings and to continue his work after his death.

The Gospel of Mary also includes a account of Mary Magdalene's visions and revelations, in which she is given special knowledge and insight into the nature of God and the spiritual realm. These visions and revelations are seen by some as a source of controversy, as they are perceived as challenging traditional Christian beliefs and teachings.

The Gospel of Mary presents a unique and distinctive perspective on the life and teachings of Jesus and the early Christian church, and it is not considered to be a reliable or authoritative source of information about these subjects. The gospels of the New Testament, particularly the gospels of Matthew, Mark, Luke, and John, are considered to be the most reliable sources of information about the life of Jesus.[35]

### What perspective does Mary present of the life of Jesus?

The Gospel of Mary presents a unique and distinctive perspective on the life of Jesus and his teachings. In the text, Jesus is depicted as a spiritual teacher who emphasizes the importance of spiritual knowledge and understanding, and who encourages his disciples to follow his teachings and to continue his work after his death.

The Gospel of Mary also includes a series of dialogues between Jesus and his disciples, in which Jesus discusses a variety of spiritual and philosophical topics, including the nature of the soul and the role of spiritual knowledge in understanding the nature of God and the spiritual realm.

The Gospel of Mary presents a perspective on the life and teachings of Jesus that is distinct from the accounts provided in the gospels of the New Testament. It is not considered to be a reliable or authoritative source of information about the life of Jesus, and its depiction of Jesus and his teachings should not be taken as definitive or authoritative. The gospels of the New Testament, particularly the gospels of Matthew, Mark, Luke, and John, are considered to be the most reliable sources of information about the life of Jesus.

### What is a summary of the series of dialogues between Jesus and his disciples in the Gospel of Mary?

The text of the Gospel of Mary consists of a series of dialogues between Jesus and his disciples, as well as a series of visions and revelations that are experienced by Mary Magdalene. In these dialogues, Jesus teaches his disciples about the nature of the soul and the importance of spiritual knowledge and understanding. He also encourages them to follow his teachings and to continue his work after his death.

Some specific themes and topics that are discussed in the dialogues between Jesus and his disciples in the Gospel of Mary include:

The nature of the soul: Jesus teaches his disciples about the nature of the soul and the importance of spiritual knowledge and understanding in understanding the nature of God and the spiritual realm.

The role of spiritual knowledge: Jesus emphasizes the importance of spiritual knowledge and understanding in attaining a deeper connection with God and the spiritual realm.

The importance of following Jesus' teachings: Jesus encourages his disciples to follow his teachings and to continue his work after his death.

The nature of the spiritual realm: Jesus discusses the nature of the spiritual realm and the role of the soul in understanding and experiencing it.

Overall, the dialogues between Jesus and his disciples in the Gospel of Mary present a unique and distinctive perspective on the life and teachings of Jesus, and they should not be considered a reliable or definitive source of information about his life or teachings. The gospels of the New Testament, particularly the gospels of Matthew, Mark, Luke, and John, are considered to be the most reliable sources of information about the life of Jesus.

**How is the Gospel of Mary teachings different from the synoptic Gospels in the Holy bible?**

The gospels of the New Testament, particularly the gospels of Matthew, Mark, Luke, and John, are considered to be the most reliable sources of information about the life of Jesus. These texts are known as the synoptic gospels because they contain many similarities in terms of their content and structure. They are considered to be part of the canon of the Christian Bible and are considered to be authoritative and definitive accounts of the life and teachings of Jesus.[36]

The Gospel of Mary presents a unique and distinctive perspective on the life and teachings of Jesus that is different from the accounts provided in the synoptic gospels. It includes a series of dialogues between

Jesus and his disciples, as well as a series of visions and revelations that are experienced by Mary Magdalene. In these dialogues, Jesus teaches his disciples about the nature of the soul and the importance of spiritual knowledge and understanding. He also encourages them to follow his teachings and to continue his work after his death.

While the Gospel of Mary includes some information about the life and teachings of Jesus, it should not be considered a reliable or definitive source of information about these subjects. The gospels of the New Testament, particularly the gospels of Matthew, Mark, Luke, and John, are considered to be the most reliable sources of information about the life of Jesus.

## What information about the life of Jesus is unique in the Gospel of Mary?

The Gospel of Mary presents a unique and distinctive perspective on the life and teachings of Jesus that is different from the accounts provided in the synoptic gospels of the New Testament. It includes a series of dialogues between Jesus and his disciples, as well as a series of visions and revelations that are experienced by Mary Magdalene. In these dialogues, Jesus teaches his disciples about the nature of the soul and the importance of spiritual knowledge and understanding. He also encourages them to follow his teachings and to continue his work after his death.

Some specific pieces of information about the life of Jesus that are unique to the Gospel of Mary include:

The emphasis on the importance of spiritual knowledge and understanding: In the Gospel of Mary, Jesus emphasizes the importance of spiritual knowledge and understanding in attaining a deeper connection with God and the spiritual realm.

The depiction of Mary Magdalene as a key figure in the early Christian church: In the Gospel of Mary, Mary Magdalene is depicted as a key figure in the early Christian church and as a recipient of special knowledge and insight from Jesus.

The portrayal of Jesus as a spiritual teacher: In the Gospel of Mary, Jesus is depicted as a spiritual teacher who emphasizes the importance of spiritual knowledge and understanding, and who encourages his disciples to follow his teachings and to continue his work after his death.

While the Gospel of Mary includes some unique pieces of information about the life of Jesus, it should not be considered a reliable or definitive source of information about his life or teachings. The gospels of the New Testament, particularly the gospels of Matthew, Mark, Luke, and John, are considered to be the most reliable sources of information about the life of Jesus.

### How is Mary Magdalene depicted as a key figure in the early Christian Church in the Gospel of Mary?[37]

In the Gospel of Mary, Mary Magdalene is depicted as a key figure in the early Christian church and as a recipient of special knowledge and insight from Jesus. She is portrayed as one of Jesus' closest and most trusted disciples, and she is depicted as having a deep understanding of his teachings.[38]

According to the Gospel of Mary, Mary Magdalene experiences a series of visions and revelations that give her special knowledge and insight into the nature of God and the spiritual realm. These visions and revelations are seen by some as a source of controversy, as they are perceived as challenging traditional Christian beliefs and teachings.

The Gospel of Mary portrays Mary Magdalene as a key figure in the early Christian church; needless to say, it should not be considered a reliable or definitive source of information about the life of Jesus or the early Christian church. The gospels of the New Testament, particularly the gospels of Matthew, Mark, Luke, and John, are considered to be the most reliable sources of information about the life of Jesus and the early Christian church.

If the Gospel of Mary was included in the canon, would this give evidence of woman ordination in the catholic church?

# INEFFABILIS A SYSTEMATIC ANALYSIS OF APOCRYPHAL LITERATURE & CRITIQUE OF NON-CANONICAL TEXTS

The Gospel of Mary is a non-canonical text that purports to provide additional information about the life of Jesus and the teachings of the early Christian church. It is not considered to be a reliable historical source, and it is not considered to be part of the canon of the Christian Bible.

If the Gospel of Mary were included in the canon of the Christian Bible, it is unlikely that it would provide any evidence of woman ordination in the Catholic Church. The canon of the Christian Bible includes the Old Testament, which is the Hebrew Bible, and the New Testament, which contains the gospels of Matthew, Mark, Luke, and John, as well as other texts that describe the teachings and activities of Jesus and the early Christian church.

The Gospel of Mary is not considered to be a reliable or authoritative source of information about the life of Jesus or the early Christian church, and it should not be taken as definitive or authoritative in matters of Christian doctrine or practice. The gospels of the New Testament, particularly the gospels of Matthew, Mark, Luke, and John, are considered to be the most reliable sources of information about the life of Jesus and the teachings of the early Christian church.

The inclusion of the Gospel of Mary in the canon of the Christian Bible would not provide any evidence of woman ordination in the Catholic Church. The Catholic Church's teachings on the ordination of women are based on a variety of sources and traditions, including the teachings of Jesus and the practices of the early Christian church. The Gospel of Mary is not considered to be a reliable or authoritative source of information on these matters.

# Chapter 8 women & Ordiination

The idea of the Gospel of Mary can make one wonder about the evidence of women and ordination in the Holy Bible.

**What evidence of female deacons is there in the Holy Bible?**

The Bible mentions several women who held leadership roles in the early Christian church, including the office of deacon. The word "deacon" comes from the Greek word "diakonos," which means "servant" or "minister." Deacons in the Christian church are ordained leaders who assist the clergy and serve the needs of the community.[39]

There are several passages in the New Testament that mention women who held the office of deacon in the early Christian church. For example, in the book of Romans, Paul mentions Phoebe as a deacon of the church in Cenchreae: "I commend to you our sister Phoebe, a deacon of the church at Cenchreae" (Romans 16:1). In the book of 1 Timothy, Paul instructs Timothy to ordain qualified men and women as deacons: "Therefore an overseer must be above reproach, the husband of one wife, sober-minded, self-controlled, respectable, hospitable, able to teach, not a drunkard, not violent but gentle, not quarrelsome, not a lover of money. He must manage his own household well, with all dignity keeping his children submissive, for if someone does not know how to manage his own household, how will he care for God's church? He must not be a recent convert, or he may become puffed up with conceit and fall into the condemnation of the devil. Moreover, he must be well thought of by outsiders, so that he may not fall into disgrace, into a snare of the devil" (1 Timothy 3:2-7).

These passages provide evidence that women were ordained as deacons in the early Christian church and played important roles in the ministry and leadership of the church. However, it is important to note that the role of deacon in the modern Catholic Church is typically understood to be open only to men. The Catholic Church's teachings on the ordination of women are based on a variety of sources and traditions, including the teachings of Jesus and the practices of the early Christian church.

**If women are ordained deacons in the Catholic church, would this open the doors as priest?**

The Catholic Church currently ordains men to the priesthood and not women to the diaconate (the office of deacon). Additionally, women are not ordained to the priesthood in the Catholic Church. The Catholic Church's teaching on the ordination of women to the priesthood is based on a variety of sources and traditions, including the teachings of Jesus and the practices of the early Christian church.

In the Catholic Church, the priesthood is understood to be a participation in the ministry of Jesus as a member of the ordained clergy. Priests are responsible for celebrating the sacraments, especially the Eucharist, and for proclaiming the Gospel and teaching the faith. The Catholic Church teaches that the priesthood is a specific vocation that is open only to men.[40]

The diaconate, on the other hand, is a ministry of service within the Church. Deacons are ordained to assist the clergy and to serve the needs of the community. In the Catholic Church, the diaconate is open to only men. However, there is currently a study to verify the claim that women were historically deacons in the Holy Bible. If this is proved, women could possibly be ordained deacons in the future. Deacons may be ordained to the diaconate as a permanent state, or they may be ordained on a temporary basis as a step towards ordination to the priesthood. The likely hood that women being ordained as priest if the office of the diaconate is open to women is slim to none.

The Catholic Church's teaching on the ordination of women to the priesthood is that it is not possible. The Church teaches that the priesthood is a specific vocation that is open only to men.

# Chapter 9 The "holy quran" and Jesus

**What does the holy Koran say about Jesus?**

Previous mentions of the Gospel of Mary brought out the fact that Jesus is mentioned in the Holy Quran. The Qur'an, also spelled Quran or Koran, is the sacred text of Islam and is considered by Muslims to be the word of God as revealed to the prophet Muhammad. The Qur'an contains many references to Jesus, who is revered as a prophet in Islam and is known in Arabic as "Isa."

According to the Qur'an, Jesus was born to the Virgin Mary through the intervention of the Holy Spirit. He is described as a prophet and messenger of God, and he is believed to have performed many miracles during his lifetime. The Qur'an also speaks of Jesus' death and resurrection, and it asserts that he was not crucified but was instead taken up into heaven by God.[41]

In the Qur'an, Jesus is revered as a prophet and is considered to be one of the greatest prophets of God, along with Abraham, Moses, and Muhammad. He is often mentioned in the Qur'an alongside other prophets, and he is seen as a source of guidance and inspiration for Muslims.[42]

The Qur'an presents a positive view of Jesus and acknowledges his important role in the history of salvation. However, it also asserts that Jesus is not the Son of God and that he is not divine. According to Islamic belief, God is unique and transcendent, and it is not possible for a human being to be equal to or part of God in any way.

**Does the Qur'an reference about Jesus come from any of the text that are considered lost books of the bible?**

The Qur'an is the sacred text of Islam and is considered by Muslims to be the word of God as revealed to the prophet Muhammad. It is not based on any of the texts that are considered "lost books" of the Bible.

The concept of "lost books" of the Bible refers to texts that were written in the ancient world but are not included in the canon of any Christian denomination. These texts are often referred to as "apocryphal" or "pseudepigraphal" texts and include works such as the Gospel of Thomas, the Apocalypse of Peter, and the Acts of Paul.

The Qur'an does not reference these texts or rely on them as sources of information about the life of Jesus or the teachings of the early Christian church. Instead, the Qur'an is based on revelations that were received by the prophet Muhammad and recorded in the Arabic language.

The Qur'an is a distinct and independent text that is not based on the "lost books" of the Bible or any other non-canonical texts. It is considered by Muslims to be the word of God as revealed to Muhammad, and it is a central and authoritative source of guidance and inspiration for the Islamic faith

# Chapter 10 The Unchanged canon

**Why haven't any new books been added to the cannon over the years?**

The canon of the Bible, both Old and New Testaments, has remained largely unchanged for centuries. While a few minor variations exist between Christian denominations and branches, the core of the canon has remained consistent. But why hasn't any new book been added to the canon over the years? There are several factors to consider.

Firstly, the canonization process was a long and complex one. The books that make up the Old and New Testaments were written over many centuries and by numerous authors, and they were not compiled into a single collection until centuries after the last book was written. The process of canonization involved a careful examination of each book to ensure that it was consistent with established doctrine and that it had been written under divine inspiration. This process took place over several centuries and involved numerous councils and discussions among early Christian leaders.[43]

Secondly, the early church fathers placed great emphasis on the apostolic origin of the texts included in the canon. This meant that the books included in the Bible were believed to have been written either by the apostles themselves or by close associates of the apostles. Since the apostles lived in the first century AD, no new books could be added to the canon after this time.

Thirdly, the canon of the Bible has been recognized and accepted by the majority of Christian communities around the world. While there have been some differences in opinion regarding the inclusion of certain books, the core of the canon has remained consistent. As such, there has been little impetus to add new books to the canon.

Finally, there have been some books written over the years that claim to be divinely inspired and have sought inclusion in the canon. However, these books have not been accepted by the majority of Christian communities, often due to their inconsistent or incompatible teachings with established doctrine. These books are generally referred to as apocryphal or pseudepigraphal, meaning that they are not considered to be authentic or authoritative.

The canonization process was a long and complex one, and the books included in the Bible have been recognized and accepted by the majority of Christian communities for centuries. While there have been some attempts to add new books to the canon, these have generally not been successful due to a variety of factors.

### What are the factors that have prevented new books being added to the canon?

The canon of the Bible is the collection of sacred texts that are considered to be authoritative and inspired by God within the Christian faith. The canon has been established over a long period of time and is generally considered to be closed, meaning that no new books have been added to it since the early centuries of Christianity. There are several factors that have contributed to this, including historical, theological, and practical reasons.

One of the primary factors that has prevented new books from being added to the canon is historical in nature. The books that are included in the canon were written during the first few centuries of Christianity, and were generally accepted as authoritative by the early Christian communities. These texts were widely circulated and used in worship services, and were considered to be essential for Christian faith and practice. However, as Christianity spread and developed over time, new texts emerged that claimed to be inspired by God and authoritative for Christian belief and practice. These texts were often controversial and debated within the early Christian communities, and ultimately many of them were rejected as heretical or lacking in authenticity.

Another factor that has prevented new books from being added to the canon is theological in nature. The books that are included in the canon were chosen based on their theological content and their ability to convey the message of salvation through Jesus Christ. These texts were considered to be inspired by God and to contain the essential teachings of the Christian faith. However, new texts that emerged often contained theological ideas that were considered to be incompatible with Christian orthodoxy, and were therefore rejected by the early church. For example, the Gnostic texts that were popular in the early Christian communities contained ideas that were considered to be heretical, such as the belief that the material world was inherently evil and that salvation was achieved through secret knowledge.

Practical reasons have also played a role in preventing new books from being added to the canon. The process of canonization was a lengthy and complex one, and involved a great deal of debate and discussion among early Christian communities. The early church fathers were very selective about the books that were included in the canon, and only those texts that were widely accepted as authoritative and inspired by God were ultimately included. The canon was also closed at a time when the church was beginning to establish itself as a powerful institution, and adding new books to the canon could have undermined the authority of the church and caused confusion among the faithful.

The canon of the Bible has remained closed for centuries due to a combination of historical, theological, and practical factors. The books that are included in the canon were chosen based on their theological content and their ability to convey the message of salvation through Jesus Christ. New texts that emerged were often rejected as heretical or lacking in authenticity, and adding new books to the canon could have undermined the authority of the church and caused confusion among the faithful. While there have been many important religious texts that have been written since the establishment of the canon, they are generally not considered to be on the same level of authority as the books that are included in the canon chapter ten text here.

# Chapter 11 Similarities between Hindu and the Cannon

The Hindu religion has a rich history of sacred texts, many of which are considered to be similar to books in the canon of other religions such as the Bible. Hindu scriptures are often classified into two broad categories: Shruti and Smriti. Shruti refers to the Vedas, which are considered to be divine revelation, and Smriti refers to the secondary texts that are based on the Vedas but are authored by humans.

One of the most well-known Hindu texts is the Bhagavad Gita, which is part of the epic poem, the Mahabharata. The Bhagavad Gita is a dialogue between Lord Krishna and the warrior Arjuna, who is hesitant to fight in a battle. Lord Krishna teaches Arjuna about the nature of reality and the importance of fulfilling one's duty, and the text has been revered as a spiritual guide for millennia. The Bhagavad Gita is considered to be similar to the wisdom literature in the Bible, such as the Book of Proverbs.

Another important Hindu text is the Ramayana, which tells the story of the prince Rama and his journey to rescue his wife Sita from the demon king Ravana. The Ramayana is considered to be similar to the epic literature in the Bible, such as the Book of Genesis.[44]

The Upanishads are another set of important Hindu texts, which contain philosophical and spiritual teachings. They are considered to be similar to the wisdom literature in the Bible, such as the Book of Ecclesiastes.

The Puranas are a set of texts that describe the lives and deeds of various Hindu gods and goddesses. They are considered to be similar to the historical and prophetic books in the Bible, such as the Books of Kings and the Book of Daniel.

Overall, Hindu scriptures share many similarities with books in the canon of other religions, including the Bible. They contain teachings about morality, spirituality, and the nature of reality, and are revered as sacred texts that provide guidance and insight into the divine.

# Chapter 12 Similarities Between Ancient Egypt & Christianity

The religion of ancient Egypt is often considered one of the oldest and most influential belief systems in the world, having lasted for thousands of years before the arrival of Christianity. While there are many differences between the two religions, there are also some similarities that can be drawn.

One of the most notable similarities is the concept of resurrection. In ancient Egypt, it was believed that the god Osiris had died and then risen again, and that this event allowed for the possibility of resurrection for all people. Similarly, in Christianity, the resurrection of Jesus is seen as a central event that allows for the possibility of eternal life for believers.

Another similarity is the concept of judgment after death. In ancient Egypt, it was believed that after death, the soul of the deceased would be judged by the god Osiris and his council. In Christianity, the concept of judgment after death is also present, with the idea of a final judgment at the end of time when all souls will be judged based on their actions during life.[45]

Additionally, both religions have a complex hierarchy of deities, with various gods and goddesses holding different levels of power and influence. In ancient Egypt, the pharaoh was seen as a divine ruler and often considered a god in his own right. In Christianity, there is a hierarchy of saints and angels, with God considered the ultimate ruler of the universe.

There are also similarities in the way that both religions use sacred texts. In ancient Egypt, there were various texts considered sacred, including the Book of the Dead, which contained spells and prayers intended to guide the soul of the deceased through the afterlife. In Christianity, the Bible is considered the ultimate authority on faith and morals.

However, it is important to note that while there are some similarities between ancient Egyptian religion and Christianity, there are also many differences. For example, in ancient Egypt, there was a belief in multiple gods and goddesses, while Christianity is monotheistic. Additionally, the nature of the afterlife and the concept of sin and salvation are different in the two religions.

While there are some similarities between ancient Egyptian religion and Christianity, there are also many differences. Both religions have complex belief systems that have influenced their followers for thousands of years, and each has its own unique set of practices, rituals, and sacred texts.

The ancient religion of Ethiopia, often referred to as the Ethiopian Orthodox Tewahedo Church, shares many similarities with Christianity. The religion has its roots in the ancient Kingdom of Aksum, which was located in what is now Ethiopia and Eritrea. The Ethiopian Orthodox Church has its own scriptures, liturgical language, and distinct practices that have been influenced by its unique history and cultural heritage.

One of the most significant similarities between Ethiopian religion and Christianity is the belief in a single God who is the creator and sustainer of the universe. This belief is central to both religions, and in Ethiopia, God is often referred to as "Abba," which means father. Another similarity is the belief in the afterlife, with both religions teaching that the soul continues to exist after death and that the ultimate destination of the soul is determined by the life one leads on earth.

The Ethiopian Orthodox Church also has many practices that are similar to Christianity. For example, baptism is an important sacrament in both religions, and Ethiopian Orthodox Christians believe in the Holy Trinity, the divinity of Christ, and the resurrection. Both religions also celebrate holidays that are rooted in the same religious traditions, such as Easter and Christmas.

# INEFFABILIS A SYSTEMATIC ANALYSIS OF APOCRYPHAL LITERATURE & CRITIQUE OF NON-CANONICAL TEXTS

The Ethiopian Orthodox Church has its own set of scriptures, which includes the Old and New Testaments, as well as several books that are unique to the Ethiopian Orthodox Church. These include the Book of Enoch and the Book of Jubilees, which are considered apocryphal by many Christians but are accepted as canonical by the Ethiopian Orthodox Church.

The Ethiopian Orthodox Church also has its own liturgical language, Ge'ez, which is used during religious services. Ge'ez is an ancient language that has been used in Ethiopia for thousands of years, and it is closely related to the ancient Semitic languages of Hebrew and Arabic. The use of Ge'ez during religious services gives the Ethiopian Orthodox Church a distinctive character that sets it apart from other Christian churches.

The ancient religion of Ethiopia, as practiced by the Ethiopian Orthodox Tewahedo Church, shares many similarities with Christianity. Both religions share a belief in a single God, the afterlife, and important sacraments such as baptism. The Ethiopian Orthodox Church also has its own unique scriptures, liturgical language, and practices that reflect the country's rich cultural heritage

# Chapter 13 Revelation of God

The Revelation of God shows through all major religions be it monotheistic or polytheistic.

Throughout human history, people have been searching for answers to life's big questions, such as the meaning of existence and the nature of the divine. One way in which people have sought answers is through religion, and there are many different religions in the world. While these religions may seem vastly different on the surface, there are often underlying similarities that suggest a common source of inspiration or revelation.

One common thread among many religions is the belief in a higher power or powers that guide and shape the world. Monotheistic religions, such as Judaism, Christianity, and Islam, believe in one all-powerful God who is the creator of the universe and the source of all goodness. Polytheistic religions, such as Hinduism, believe in multiple gods and goddesses who govern different aspects of the world and influence human affairs. Nyord, R. (2018). 'Taking ancient Egyptian mortuary religion seriously': Why would we, and how could we? Journal of Ancient Egyptian Interconnections, 17(1).[46]

Despite the apparent differences in these beliefs, there are many similarities in the way that the divine is revealed to humanity. In monotheistic religions, God often reveals himself through prophets or messengers, who convey his word and will to the people. In the Jewish and Christian traditions, for example, God revealed himself through figures such as Abraham, Moses, and Jesus, while in Islam, God revealed himself through the prophet Muhammad.

Similarly, in polytheistic religions, there are often stories of gods and goddesses who communicate with humans and guide them on their path. In Hinduism, for example, there are many stories of gods and goddesses who interact with humans and impart wisdom and guidance. In some cases, these stories are seen as allegorical, with the gods representing different aspects of human nature or the divine.

Another way in which the revelation of God shows through all major religions is through moral teachings. Many religions share similar values and principles, such as the importance of compassion, justice, and humility. These values are often expressed through religious texts and teachings, which are seen as sacred and authoritative.

Despite the similarities among religions, there are also many differences, and it is important to respect and appreciate these differences. Each religion has its own unique history and cultural context, and each offers its own perspective on the nature of the divine and the purpose of human existence. However, by recognizing the commonalities that exist among different religions, we can gain a deeper appreciation for the diversity of human spirituality and the many ways in which people have sought to understand the divine.

**What does the revelation of God reveal to us through the lost books of the bible?**

The lost books of the Bible, also known as the apocryphal or non-canonical texts, provide us with a unique perspective on the revelation of God. While these texts were not included in the official canon of the Bible, they can still be a valuable source of insight into the beliefs and practices of early Christian communities, as well as the broader cultural and religious context in which Christianity emerged.

One important way in which the lost books of the Bible reveal the nature of God is through their portrayal of Jesus. For example, the Gospel of Thomas presents Jesus as a teacher of wisdom, whose teachings emphasize the importance of self-knowledge and inner transformation. The Gospel of Mary Magdalene portrays Jesus as a spiritual guide who encourages his followers to seek the divine within themselves. These depictions of Jesus are distinct from those found in the canonical gospels, and offer a more nuanced understanding of Jesus' teachings and mission.

The lost books of the Bible also provide insight into the early Christian community's understanding of salvation and the afterlife. For example, the Apocalypse of Peter describes a series of visions in which Peter is shown the torments that await sinners in the afterlife, while the Gospel of Judas portrays Judas not as a traitor, but as a disciple who is entrusted with a special knowledge of the divine plan for salvation.

Additionally, some of the lost books of the Bible offer a glimpse into the role of women in early Christianity. The Gospel of Mary Magdalene, for example, portrays Mary as a close confidante and spiritual leader among Jesus' disciples, while the Acts of Paul and Thecla describes a woman who converts to Christianity and becomes an influential evangelist in her own right.

Overall, the lost books of the Bible offer a window into the diversity of beliefs and practices within early Christianity, as well as the broader religious and cultural context in which Christianity emerged. By studying these texts, we can gain a deeper understanding of the ways in which people have sought to understand and connect with the divine throughout history, and how those understandings continue to shape our spiritual and cultural landscape today

**How would the cannon be different if some of the lost books of the bible were included? How would Jesus be viewed differently?**

The Christian canon, as it exists today, was established over several centuries and reflects the beliefs and traditions of the early Christian communities. While the canonized books of the Bible provide a comprehensive account of the life, teachings, and ministry of Jesus, there are also many non-canonical texts that shed light on his life and teachings.

If some of the lost books of the Bible were included in the canon, it would have a significant impact on the way Jesus is viewed and understood by Christians. For example, the Gospel of Mary Magdalene, which was not included in the canon, depicts Mary as a prominent disciple of Jesus and contains teachings and insights that are not found in the canonical gospels. If this gospel was included, it would give greater recognition to Mary Magdalene as an important figure in the early Christian movement and challenge traditional views about the role of women in the church.

Similarly, if the Gospel of Thomas was included in the canon, it would add a unique perspective to Jesus' teachings and emphasize the importance of personal spiritual discovery and inner wisdom. This gospel contains a collection of sayings of Jesus, some of which are not found in the canonical gospels, and places a greater emphasis on the individual's relationship with God rather than on organized religion.

Other lost books of the Bible, such as the Gospel of Judas, provide alternative interpretations of the life and teachings of Jesus. This gospel depicts Judas not as a traitor, but as a close confidant of Jesus who was entrusted with a special knowledge that the other disciples did not possess. If this gospel was included in the canon, it would challenge traditional views about Judas and could potentially change the way he is viewed in Christian theology.

In addition to these specific examples, the inclusion of lost books in the canon could also lead to a broader understanding of the diversity of early Christian thought and belief. It could provide insights into the various sects and movements that existed in the early church and challenge the idea of a singular, unified Christian doctrine.

However, it is important to note that the process of canonization was a complex and lengthy one, and the books that were ultimately included in the canon were selected based on a variety of factors, including their widespread use and acceptance by the early Christian communities, their theological consistency with other texts, and their authority and authorship. Therefore, it is impossible to predict exactly how the canon would be different if some of the lost books were included, but it is likely that it would provide a richer and more complex understanding of the life and teachings of Jesus.

# Chapter 14 Conclusion

The concept of the universal revelation of God refers to the idea that God has revealed divine truths to humanity through a variety of means throughout history. These revelations can be found not only in the canonical texts of various religions, but also in other sources, such as literature, art, and philosophy.

If we accept the notion of the universal revelation of God, it can help foster a sense of communion between people of all faiths. This is because it recognizes that God's truth is not limited to one particular religion or tradition, but rather is available to all people who seek it. By recognizing the commonalities that exist between various religious traditions, we can begin to break down barriers and promote a sense of unity and understanding.

One way in which the universal revelation of God can foster communion between people of different faiths is by encouraging us to focus on the shared values that are present in all religions. For example, most religions teach the importance of compassion, love, and respect for others. By emphasizing these shared values, we can help to promote understanding and respect between different faith communities.

Another way in which the universal revelation of God can foster communion is by promoting dialogue and collaboration between people of different faiths. By engaging in respectful dialogue, we can learn from one another and deepen our understanding of our own faith and the faith of others. By working together on common goals, such as promoting social justice or protecting the environment, we can build bridges of understanding and respect.

The inclusion of lost books of the Bible, as well as other religious texts, can also help foster a deeper sense of communion between people of different faiths. By exploring these texts, we can gain a greater understanding of the diverse ways in which people have experienced and understood God throughout history. This can help us appreciate the richness and diversity of different religious traditions, and can deepen our respect for the beliefs and practices of others.[47]

In conclusion, the concept of the universal revelation of God has the potential to foster communion and understanding between people of all faiths. By recognizing the commonalities that exist between different religions, and by engaging in respectful dialogue and collaboration, we can build bridges of understanding and respect that can help us to live in greater harmony with one another.

[1] Platt, R. H. (Ed.). (1927). The Lost Books of the Bible and the Forgotten Books of Eden. World Pub.

[2] Carson, D. A. (1997). The Apocryphal/Deuterocanonical Books: An Evangelical View. The Parallel Apocrypha.

[3] Collins, J. J. (2014). The Penumbra of the Canon. What Do the Deuterocanonical Books Represent?. Canonicity, Setting, Wisdom in the Deuterocanonicals, 225, 1-17.

[4] Gathercole, S. J. (2014). The Gospel of Thomas: Introduction and Commentary. Brill.

[5] Miller, J. P. (2018). Zen and the Gospel of Thomas. Simon and Schuster.

[6] Miller, J. P. (2018). Zen and the Gospel of Thomas. Simon and Schuster.

[7] DeConick, A. D. (2006). Recovering the original Gospel of Thomas: A history of the Gospel and its growth (Vol. 286). A&C Black.

[8] Valantasis, R. (1999). Is the Gospel of Thomas ascetical? Revisiting an old problem with a new theory. Journal of Early Christian Studies, 7(1), 55-81.

[9] Säve-Söderbergh, T. (1967). Gnostic and canonical gospel traditions:(with special reference to the Gospel of Thomas). In The Origins of Gnosticism/Le origini dello gnosticismo (pp. 552-562). Brill.

[10] Davies, S. L. (2004). The Gospel of Thomas and Christian Wisdom. Bardic Press.

[11] Kasser, R., Meyer, M., Wurst, G., & Gaudard, F. (Eds.). (2008). The gospel of Judas. National Geographic Books.

[12] Gathercole, S. (2007). The Gospel of Judas. The Expository Times, 118(5), 209-215.

[13] Pagels, E. H., & King, K. L. (2007). Reading Judas: the Gospel of Judas and the shaping of Christianity. Penguin.

[14] Kasser, R., Meyer, M., Wurst, G., & Gaudard, F. (Eds.). (2008). The gospel of Judas. National Geographic Books.

[15] Ehrman, B. D. (2008). The Lost Gospel of Judas Iscariot: A new look at betrayer and betrayed. Oxford University Press.

[16] Gathercole, S. J. (2014). The Gospel of Thomas: Introduction and Commentary. Brill.

[17] Piovanelli, P. (2010). Thomas in Edessa? Another Look at the Original Setting of the Gospel of Thomas. In Myths, Martyrs, and Modernity (pp. 443-461). Brill.

[18] Bremmer, J. N. (2003). The Apocalypse of Peter (Vol. 7). Peeters Publishers.

[19] Bremmer, J. N. (2003). The Apocalypse of Peter (Vol. 7). Peeters Publishers.

[20] Bremmer, J. N. (2019). The Apocalypse of Peter as the First Christian Martyr text: Its date, provenance and relationship with 2 Peter. In 2 Peter and the Apocalypse of Peter: Towards a New Perspective (pp. 75-98). Brill.

[21] Bauckham, R. (1985). The Two Fig Tree Parables in the Apocalypse of Peter. Journal of Biblical Literature, 104(2), 269-287.

[22] Bremmer, J. N. (Ed.). (1998). The Apocryphal Acts of Peter: Magic, Miracles and Gnosticism (Vol. 3). Peeters Publishers.

[23] Steinová, E. (2014). The prehistory of the Latin Acts of Peter (BHL 6663) and the Latin Acts of Paul (BHL 6575). Some observations about the development of the Virtutes apostolorum. The Apocryphal Acts of the Apostles in Latin Christianity: Proceedings of the First International Summer School on Christian Apocryphal Literature (ISCAL), Strasbourg, 24-27 June 2012, 69-84.

[24] Thomas, C. M. (1997). Canon and antitype: The relationship between the Acts of Peter and the New Testament. Semeia, (80), 185.

[25] Thomas, C. M. (2003). The Acts of Peter, Gospel Literature, and the Ancient Novel: Rewriting the Past. Oxford University Press on Demand.

[26] Thomas, C. M. (2003). The Acts of Peter, Gospel Literature, and the Ancient Novel: Rewriting the Past. Oxford University Press on Demand.

[27] Chartrand-Burke, T. (2008). The Infancy Gospel of Thomas. The non-canonical gospels, 126-38.

[28] Chartrand-Burke, T. (2008). The Infancy Gospel of Thomas. The non-canonical gospels, 126-38.

[29] Bockmuehl, M. (2018). Scriptural Completion in the Infancy Gospel of James. Pro Ecclesia, 27(2), 180-202.

[30] Hawk, B. W. (2020). The Gospel of Pseudo-Matthew and the Nativity of Mary. The Gospel of Pseudo-Matthew and the Nativity of Mary, 1-100

[31] The Armenian Gospel of the Infancy: with three early versions of the Protevangelium of James. Oxford University Press on Demand, 2008

[32] Horn, C. B. (2007). Mary between Bible and Qur'an: Soundings into the transmission and reception history of the Protoevangelium of James on the basis of selected literary sources in coptic and copto-arabic and of art-historical evidence pertaining to Egypt. Islam and Christian–Muslim Relations, 18(4), 509-538.

[33] Hawk, B. W. (2020). The Gospel of Pseudo-Matthew and the Nativity of Mary. The Gospel of Pseudo-Matthew and the Nativity of Mary, 1-100.

[34] Tuckett, C. (2007). The gospel of Mary. The Expository Times, 118(8), 365-371.

[35] Tuckett, C. (2012). The Gospel of Mary. Revista catalana de teologia, 111-129.

[36] Horn, C. B. (2007). Mary between Bible and Qur'an: Soundings into the transmission and reception history of the Protoevangelium of James on the basis of selected literary sources in coptic and copto-arabic and of art-historical evidence pertaining to Egypt. Islam and Christian–Muslim Relations, 18(4), 509-538.

[37] Tuckett, C. (2007). The gospel of Mary. The Expository Times, 118(8), 365-371.

[38] King, K. L. (1998). 1. Prophetic Power and Women's Authority: The Case of the Gospel of Mary (Magdalene). In Women Preachers and Prophets through Two Millennia of Christianity (pp. 21-41). University of California Press.

[39] Madigan, K., & Osiek, C. (Eds.). (2005). Ordained women in the early church: A documentary history. JHU Press.

[40] Scanlon, R., & Cap, O. F. M. (1996). Women Deacons: At What Price?. Homiletic and Pastoral Review XCVI, 10, 6-14.

[41] Ali, M. M. (2011). Holy Quran. Ahmadiyya Anjuman Ishaat Islam Lahore USA.

[42] Larson, W. (2008). Jesus in Islam and Christianity: Discussing the Similarities and the Differences. Missiology, 36(3), 327-341.

[43] Gallagher, S. V. (2001). Contingencies and intersections: the formation of pedagogical canons. Pedagogy, 1(1), 53-67.

[44] Norris, J., Carvalho, L. M., Jones, C., & Cannon, F. (2015). WRF simulations of two extreme snowfall events associated with contrasting extratropical cyclones over the western and central Himalaya. Journal of Geophysical Research: Atmospheres, 120(8), 3114-3138.

[45] Assmann, J. (2002). Resurrection in ancient Egypt.

[46] Jensen, P. (2002). The revelation of God. InterVarsity Press

[47] Goldsworthy, G. (2002). According to plan: The unfolding revelation of God in the Bible. InterVarsity Press.

# Don't miss out!

Visit the website below and you can sign up to receive emails whenever Anthony Brown publishes a new book. There's no charge and no obligation.

https://books2read.com/r/B-A-CONCB-CCQTC

BOOKS2READ

Connecting independent readers to independent writers.

Did you love *Ineffabilis A Systematic Analysis of Apocryphal Literature & Critique of Non-Canonical Texts*? Then you should read *Democracy in Crisis. The Challenges Facing America in the 21st Century*[1] by Anthony Wayne Brown!

This is the sixth book for Anthony W. Brown. The first book, "Rebirth from Darkness to Light", was written under the pseudonym, Just Anthony, which is the authors stage name as a poet. The second book, " Hope Peace, Love & Joy, An Inquiry into their Philosophical Nature and the Endless Pursuit of Attaining Them" is a book written Christmas of 2022 and rebranded under the current title in 2023. This book is an intersection between Counseling Psychology and religion. Other books written by the author are " Ineffabillis A Systematic Analysis of Apocryphal Literature & Critique of Non[Canonical Texts" and "Bearing Fruit & Living Our Faith, Strengthening Our Relationship with God through Christian Witness & Service a Catholic Catechesis for Catechized High School Students" and " From Darkness to Light, Understanding Over Coming Grief, Death and Dying".

---

1. https://books2read.com/u/mZpvnJ

2. https://books2read.com/u/mZpvnJ

Discovering the dangers that certain Political movements pose to the democracy of the United States of America in this insightful book. Through illuminating commentary and warnings, the author sheds light on the threats that persist and erode the very foundations of democracy as w4e know it.

Furthermore, this book offers a profound analysis of the deeply-rooted issue of racism in American history. It assumes that the readers possess a working knowledge of the nations' past and are aware of current events. By delving into these complex issues, the book aims to raise awareness and promote critical thinking about the challenges that American democracy faces in the 21st century.

Brown is a Life Coach & Counselor residing in the Washington DC Metropolitan area. Brown works full-time as an educator. He teaches in the public-school system and also at a local college. Brown is in private practice as a Counselor & Life Coach. Brown has a Bachelor's Degree in History with a minor in Criminal Justice from the University of Houston. Brown also studied Human Geography at Prairie View A & M University. He has a Master in Theology from the University of St. Thomas, Houston, and a Master in Counseling Psychology specializing in Marriage & Family Therapy from Houston Graduate School of Theology. Brown has also done some postgraduate work in Pastoral Care & Forensic Psychology.

# About the Author

Anthony Brown is a distinguished Life Coach and Counselor based in the Washington DC Metropolitan area. With a profound commitment to personal development, Brown serves as a dedicated educator within the public school system and imparts his knowledge at a local college. In addition to his role in education, Brown operates a thriving private practice as a Counselor & Life Coach.

Brown's academic journey is marked by excellence, holding a Bachelor's Degree in History with a minor in Criminal Justice from the prestigious University of Houston. Further enriching his understanding of human dynamics, he pursued studies in Human Geography at Prairie View A & M University. Brown is a double Master's graduate, with a Master's in Theology from the University of St. Thomas, Houston, and a Master's in Counseling Psychology specializing in Marriage & Family Therapy from the esteemed Houston Graduate School of Theology.

Elevating his expertise, Brown has engaged in postgraduate studies in both Pastoral Care and Forensic Psychology, demonstrating his ongoing commitment to enhancing his skills and knowledge in these specialized fields.

# About the Publisher

Kvng Leo Publications is a subsidiary of Browne Group of Maryland LLC

Contact Information:

Anthony Brown

Browne Group of Maryland LLC

Kvng Leo Publications

6200 Riverdale Ave Ste 300 #1010 Riverdale MD 20737 USA

anthony@anthonywaynebrown.com

1-800-217-7140

Read more at https://www.kvngleo.com.